# GOING TO AMERICA

Lilliam Hernandez

ISBN 978-1-0980-8213-0 (paperback)
ISBN 978-1-0980-8214-7 (digital)

Christian Faith Publishing, Inc.
832 Park Avenue
Meadville, PA 16335
www.christianfaithpublishing.com

Printed in the United States of America

I wish to dedicate this book in loving memory of my late father, Arnoldo C. Parrales for his hard work, struggles and enduring faith in bringing us to this country to find a better life for his family.

Until we meet again, Papa

# CHAPTER 1

# Departure

It was July 25, 1964. The long-awaited day had finally arrived. There was a lot of excitement and confusion in the air. We were going to the United States, far away to begin a new life. Our parents had left seven months earlier to find jobs and a place for us. Mamita Elisa, our maternal grandmother had stayed with us to look after us.

We would be going to Houston, Texas. A lot of thoughts were going through my eight-year-old mind. What would it be like in this new country? Would I like my teachers as much as I did here? Would we have any problems making new friends? What would the food be like? Here we had plenty of fresh fruits and vegetables grown from our own backyard. My oldest brother, Arnold, who was twelve, had already been there, but I don't recall him ever talking about it. I just prayed to God that we could adjust. I knew one thing for certain, I would miss my relatives and friends.

The airport in Managua was even more of a hustle and bustle! There were people running everywhere! There was shouting and shoving all around us. My cousin Ruby, age sixteen, would be traveling along with us to look after us on the plane. Personally, I think that was a big job for a teenager, to be looking after five children ages from twenty-two months to twelve years old! Our grandparents and a minister who was a friend of the family came with us to see us off. There were plenty of hugs, kisses, and tears. A prayer was said for God to protect our flight, and we were finally on our way.

The entire flight was an experience to be remembered. How thrilling to be able to look outside and see the clouds. It was as if you could reach out and touch them with your hands. We were treated with the best of care, the flight attendants were sweet, and they all fell in love with our baby brother, Elmer, who had a head full of curls. I was hoping Mama would give him a haircut soon, we were getting tired of saying, "He's a boy, not a girl!"

The arrival to Houston was even more exciting for us. Papa and Mama were so happy to see us again, and of course so were we! Our nine-hour-long trip was finally over! We were given a quick tour of downtown—talk about drastic changes! In my hometown, we walked everywhere: to the store, to church, to school, even to town! Here we were taken by car! My four-year-old brother Jorge was completely amazed at the size of the buildings. The tallest in our town were two or three floors, compared to one hundred or plus floors! Did I ever have some adjusting to do!

# CHAPTER 2

# Adjustments

Our first night in Houston was full of new adventures. For the first time we saw a television, it was so incredible to be sitting in my aunt's living room and watching it. If I recall correctly, I believe they were showing *The Lucy Show*! We were also introduced to the telephone, another discovery for us! You would think we had just come out of a jungle or another planet by our reactions!

Since we came in July, we were also welcomed by the worst discovery yet. The weather was unbearably hot! I never would have believed that it could get *that hot*! We all broke out in rashes within days of our arrival! I became homesick in an instant! Back home we didn't know the meaning of owning a fan, much less air conditioning; there was no need for either, I suppose it's because we were surrounded by mountains, the temperature was pleasant all year long.

Due to the fact that we came on a Saturday night, preparations had to be made for us to go to Sunday school the following morning. I recall Mama washing our best clothes, which were the ones we wore on our trip. Coming from a poor family, we didn't have too many suitable outfits for church.

Sunday morning we were up early, excited, and perhaps a little nervous. Sunday school was beautiful, we were given such a nice and warm welcome by the congregation. I knew right then and there that they would become a great big part of our lives. Our pastor, Rev. J.C. Cantu and his wife were very sweet. They actually came to our aunt's home to meet us on the night we arrived! They had three children, two daughters, and a son. The two girls were close to my age and my sister's, and the son was close to my brother Jorge's. There became a close bond right away which has remained through this day.

Papa and Mama were both working at the time in order to make ends meet. We were not quite used to that arrangement, since back home Mama never worked. Here, we had a lady come and babysit, that was not a problem for us since our parents had always taught us to respect our elders; but I have to admit that when my eighteen-year-old cousin Douglas came to take over as babysitter, our fun days began! He was a clown, he knew exactly what to do to keep us entertained. He was a good cook too. We all looked to him since he was the oldest of our cousins. He became my favorite cousin. Throughout my growing years, I learned a couple of things from him to play guitar and to draw. He was a true artist, he also designed certificates for his school, and he designed his class ring when he graduated back in Nicaragua. On February 23, 1993, Douglas passed away due to a vehicle accident. He will always be my favorite cousin.

I'm grateful to God that our family has always been a close one. We lost our father in 1991 also, and his loss and Douglas's loss has made me thankful that we were always in good terms. There are no regrets; they are both in heaven now.

# CHAPTER 3

# School

September brought a whole new adventure for us. The beginning of school was upon us. Of course going to school would not be new, the fact that we were in a completely new country would definitely bring on another change though.

Douglas had us up and ready, bright and early in the morning. There were five of us: Arnold Jr., age twelve; Ligia, ten, I followed at eight; Jorge, four; and Elmer was only twenty-two months. Of course, Elmer was far too young to go to school, but Douglas had to bring him along when we walked the five or six-block trek and then take him back with him.

The walk to school was interesting, especially when we arrived at the corner of Durham and Washington. The street seemed so strangely wide to cross, seeing a police officer stopping traffic to allow us to go across made me feel important. It was unbelievable! Here I was, walking the streets of Houston, and on my way to school! I was so excited, I could hardly wait to get there! For a moment, I felt all grown up. I forgot being nervous and afraid, oblivious to what lay ahead.

Ben Milam Elementary was on Center Street. I was in total awe, looking at the beautiful reddish-brown building. I was more amazed as I looked up at its size, I felt like an ant looking up at it. Its enormous stairs seemed to reach the sky. I wonder what everyone was thinking when they saw us trailing our way up into the building with Douglas holding a baby in his arms! Even more, I wonder what the principal thought as we huddled into her office.

I was so enthralled with the idea of starting school that I completely forgot the fact that we didn't speak English! Of course! This is America! What had I been thinking? How foolish of me! All of a sudden, all my excitement seemed to fly right out of the window! I stood there along with my siblings, trying hard to swallow the knot that slowly worked its way up my throat. I looked up at Douglas and saw how easily he was conversing with the principal. It sounded so strange, as if one was playing a tape recorder in reverse. For an instant, I wanted to dash out of the door and hide under a rock or something, but my feet wouldn't budge. They felt so heavy, as if I was glued to the floor!

The conversation suddenly came to an end. Papers were signed. The principal got up from her chair gathering papers as she made her way toward the door. We all followed behind. One by one, my brother and sister were shown to their classrooms. Jorge would be starting until the following year. Arnold started sixth grade and Ligia, third. My turn finally came; I could feel myself start to shake from nerves. My eyes were stinging so bad; I was really trying my best to fight back tears. Suddenly, we were in front of my second grade classroom. My teacher was a beautiful lady, her name was Miss Wilson. Of course, I didn't find that out until later.

I was holding tight to Douglas's hand when he smiled down at me and told me he would be coming to pick me up at two o'clock. I really didn't want to hear any of that. I just wanted to go with him, but I knew it was no use arguing. I let go of his hand and watched through watery eyes as he and my little brother walked away. I found myself all alone in a classroom full of big-eyed children staring at me and a pretty teacher looking down at me, telling me God knows what because I didn't understand a thing she said!

# CHAPTER 4

# Challenge

I came to realize that my biggest fear in this new country was not being able to speak the language. I allowed that fear to slowly take over me; it caused me to get an inferiority complex. I could not communicate with any of my classmates. Everyday at lunchtime was another problem—the kids made fun of my lunches. Mama made me tacos with homemade corn tortillas. I guess they had never seen them before. All I know is that it got to the point where I dreaded the lunch hour.

As I sit here and write about those long ago days, of those difficult times, I wonder if my brothers and sister felt as I did. Going to school had always been a joyous occasion for me. I loved every minute of it. Suddenly that was gone; I no longer wanted to go. My fears were getting the better of me. On one occasion, I remember being punished for something that I didn't do. As a matter of fact, I don't even know what the "crime" was, much less who told on me. I do know that I felt so ashamed when the teacher took me outside and hit my bottom with a paddle. I couldn't even defend myself.

After that incident, I really didn't want to go to school anymore. That teacher should have never hit me! I started skipping school then! I would go along with my brother and sister. By then, we were going on our own. I would not go in the classroom but would stay outside. After the bell rang and everyone went in, I would leave. I would walk around for a while, and finally getting tired, I would go back home. Douglas would wonder why I was home so early. I had to be honest and told him my problem. I don't know if he ever told my parents what I was doing because I did it several times. I guess he felt sorry for me and didn't say anything about it, but the day came when I had to put a stop to it.

I got up that morning as usual. My brother and sister went along with me all the way to school. I did my same little stunt. I walked back home and to my surprise, my mother was there! I don't know if the school had called her prior to that, all I know is that she was home! I had to tell her everything that had been happening to me: kids making fun of me, I couldn't communicate with anyone about my assignments, how I didn't want to go back to school.

It wasn't very long when we heard a car outside at our driveway. I looked out the window, and to my horror it was the school principal! I was so shocked, I did the first thing that came to my mind: I ran into my bedroom, got under my bed, and slid all the way against the wall! I curled myself into a ball and sobbed quietly trying not to make any sound. I could hear my mom talking with her. I don't exactly know what they were saying. I did panic, though, when I heard them coming into the room. That principal had the audacity to crawl under the bed, pull me out, and carry me to her car! I was screaming my head off and kicking up a storm! I didn't even get a chance to say bye to my mom!

I will say one thing: I never missed a day of school after that incident. An interpreter was found who began to work one-on-one with me. She was very kind and understanding. It was not very long before I was on my own. I started liking school again; I made friends. It was such a relief to be able to relax and be myself again. I wonder if that would have happened in this day and age. I assume that principal would have been sued for physical abuse or something! That was an unforgettable experience though!

# CHAPTER 5

# Holidays

As the months went by, and we all began to adjust to our new life, things began to flow smoothly. Not only did I do well in school, but I found myself liking a boy in my class. He was white, had blonde hair and blue eyes. His name was Sammie; I was crazy about him! Douglas constantly teased me about him. Not only did I care for Sammie, but I was also concerned about his spiritual well-being, so I gave him one of our church tracts which explained the way of salvation. I wasn't thinking, of course, that it was in Spanish! I wonder now if he was able to have someone translate it for him.

We spent our first Thanksgiving at my Aunt Amandita's house. I don't recall celebrating this holiday back home; it must be an American thing. The dinner table looked lovely with that big turkey and all the side dishes! What a treat we had! After dinner, we played outside with our cousins. Ada Luz was my favorite of the girls and became my best friend. She and I came a long way! Since we were little girls in Nicaragua, we always played together; we were inseparable. When she was four years old, my Aunt Amandita brought her to the States. I guess it was because they didn't have any children. After those four years, we saw each other again, and we picked up where we had left off. It was as if we had never been separated.

After Thanksgiving, of course we all looked forward to Christmas. At school, we were all excited about our program coming up, and of course our Christmas party. To be perfectly honest, the only thing I remember about the program was hearing Sammie sing a song, "Away in a Manger." That was the first time I ever heard that song. My little heart did a lot of throbbing that night.

At church, we also had a beautiful service and a play given by the adults. My father and Douglas both took part in it; we sang with the children's choir. It was all so wonderful. That year, I received my first Barbie, given to me by my Aunt Amandita. At home, we had a family gathering on Christmas Eve with lots of food, and afterward we gathered around the tree to open our presents.

Those were wonderful days, days of innocence and childhood dreams. I am always thankful to God that we were raised by Christian parents. They taught us to revere God. They not only taught it, but they also lived it. They were a good example for us. I value my Christian background; it has been a strength during hard times.

# Chapter 6

# Changes

By the beginning of the new year, we were able to communicate enough in English. It was really great to be able to speak another language. Our parents complemented us on how soon we were able to pick it up, but they always stressed that we should never forget our native tongue. At home, we spoke Spanish with them and at church as well. That is why we never forgot it, and we're able to manage both languages even to this day.

Summer came quickly. I passed to the third grade, Arnold to seventh, and Ligia to fourth. Jorge would start kindergarten; Elmer was three years old. There was also a new baby on the way, although we weren't aware of it at the time. During the summer months, Ada Luz sometimes came to stay with us, or I would go over her house and spend time with her. Douglas was no longer with us; he was with my aunt. Mom was home now.

On September 27, 1965, we got up as usual to prepare for school. Mother was preparing our lunches as usual. I remember she used to put them in paper sacks and put each of our names on them. That morning, my brother Arnold and sister Ligia were celebrating their birthday. They were born on the same day, different years. He was turning thirteen, and she was turning eleven. When we came home from school that afternoon, we were all taken by surprise as we found my father waiting to tell us that we had a new baby sister! Now there were three siblings born on the same day. Is that a big deal or what? Mom named her Olivia after a sister she had lost when she was a child. We were so excited when Dad took us to the hospital to see her; she was so tiny! It was more exciting when Mom finally came home with her from the hospital.

Another change awaited us when our parents told us that we would be moving to another neighborhood. I had grown to love this house and what of school? I would surely miss my friends and teacher. I was a little nervous about having to start over again, but at least now I could speak the language.

We all took part in helping pack our things. My parents made several trips to and from our new home until we were finally ready to go. I remember walking through our empty house. Once again I felt a knot in my throat, remembering my first day of school, my encounter with the principal, our first Christmas here. Those memories will forever be in my heart. Life has too many changes, and at my young age of nine, I had, had my share. Only God knew what lay ahead for us, but we were ready to face those challenges.

# CHAPTER 7

# New Surroundings

It didn't take very long for us to get settled in our new home—actually, they were apartments. Although I missed our previous one, I grew to like this one. The apartments had two stories; we thought that was exciting. The living room, dining room, and kitchen were on the first floor; the bedrooms and bathroom were on the second floor.

Ligia and I shared one bedroom with my two younger brothers. Arnold had his own room, and my parents shared a bedroom with Olivia, who was still a baby. As long as I can remember, my sister and I always shared rooms with our younger brothers up until she graduated and went to college. Then it was me with the two of them! I joke with my husband and tell him that to this day, I have never had my own bedroom!

We lived in these apartments for three years; then my parents found a bigger house in another neighborhood. I was going to sixth grade by then. School and church were a very important part of our lives. When I started sixth grade, I remember I would walk to school every day. I would take my youngest brother Elmer with me. He was in kindergarten then, and Mom would pick him up at noon.

I graduated from high school in 1975; we had moved once again by that time. Upon graduating from school, I went to a Bible college in El Paso, Texas, Latin American Bible Institute. I have always said that those were the best years of my life; it was like being in a "little heaven." I met a young girl from Honduras, and she became my best friend until today. We have kept in touch after all these years.

There is so much more I could write about: my marriage, my children, and now I am a grandmother to a three-year-old grandson, and there is another one on the way. God has been good to me. I have gone through some very difficult times, but He has always been there to help me and to strengthen me. This story is all about the adjustments that come when moving from one country to another. I hope that it may be of encouragement to someone who may be going through something similar.

Mom and Dad; Maria Parrales and Arnoldo C. Parrales in their youth circa 1951–52

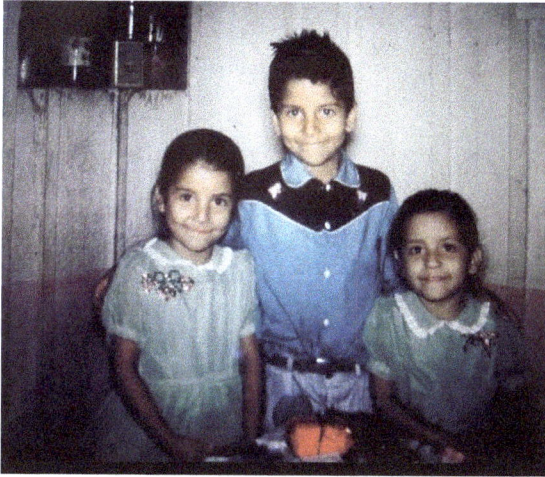

Christmas in Nicaragua 1961 or 1962

Passport picture taken in 1963

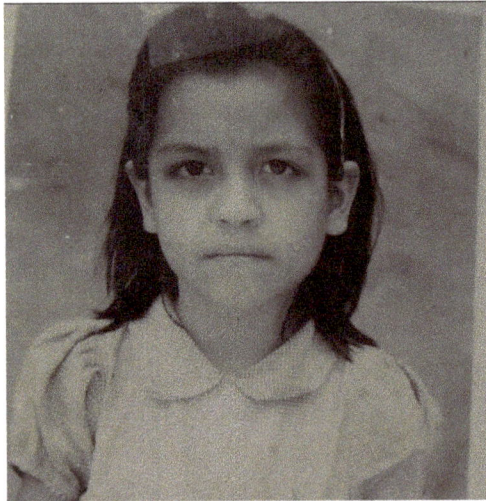

Photo from green card. 1963

Pictured at Church 1966

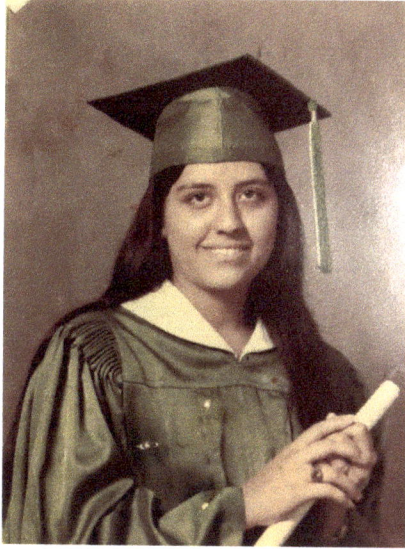

High School graduation, Stephen F. Austin 1975

At age 20, during my Bible School days 1976

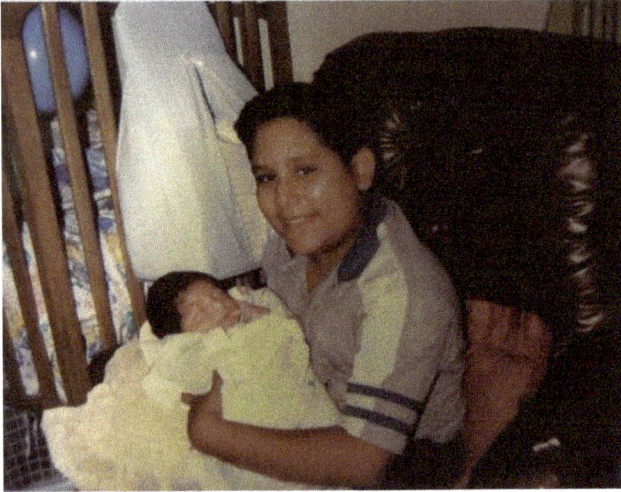

My son J. Enrique with baby brother, Johnathan 1992

With our beloved pastors, Rev., and Mrs. J.C. Cantu 1993

With my siblings, visiting one of our former houses that we lived in; 1998

With Mom at Grandmother's funeral 2001

At my son's graduation 2011

With our son Johnathan, before being deployed to Egypt 2015

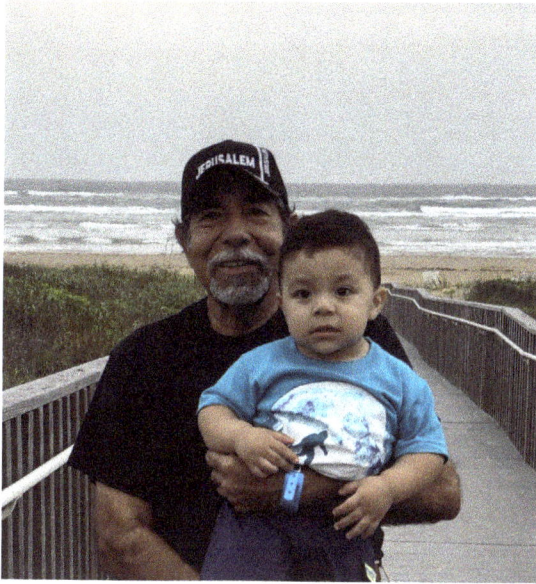

My husband with our grandson, Noah 2018

Celebrating Mom's birthday 2018

Christmas 2018

With grandson, Noah. 2020

Mom with our two grandsons, Noah age 3
and Angelo, two months old. 2020

Mom with five of her six children. 2020

# About the Author

Lilliam Hernandez is a native of Nicaragua, Central America. Her family emigrated to the US in 1964. She grew up in Houston where she graduated with honors in 1975 from Stephen F. Austin High. She has always loved to read, write, and draw; she also plays piano and guitar. Lilliam felt the need to write about her experiences of her move to this country. She is married and has two sons, one grandson, and another one on the way.

CPSIA information can be obtained
at www.ICGtesting.com
Printed in the USA
LVHW010717161222
735320LV00038B/777